CW00867744

PeacePlease

A Peaceful Way

Sue Sterling

authorHOUSE®

AuthorHouse™ UK Ltd.
500 Avebury Boulevard
Central Milton Keynes, MK9 2BE
www.authorhouse.co.uk
Phone: 08001974150

First published by AuthorHouse 11/17/2008

ISBN: 978-1-4389-1083-3 (sc)

Printed in the United States of America
Bloomington, Indiana

This book is printed on acid-free paper.

Table of Contents

1. PeacePlease and the Beginnings

Spirituality must seem a strange place to start a book called PeacePlease. But it is where it all started for me. About 15 years ago I wrote a small document of the same name, it was no more than 50 or so pages and contained thoughts on peace following a religious experience.

I sent my document to many people. To those that I thought might have the power to change the way we resolve conflicts and to those that I thought might be open to trying dialogue instead of arms. I joined the many voices that were sending out the message to stop war. I was and am sufficiently convinced of my vision for peace that I gave my simple message to anyone that would listen. I sent it to religious and political leaders and any leader or persons in a position of power, who might be inspired themselves to listen and find their way to peace. I had some replies but for the most part I left it with whoever I wrote to, to respond themselves or not. It was a free message of encouragement.

What I said was, 'Wake Up Peace Is Possible'. The message I gave was for Ordinary folk who just wanted peace and for some, what I said seemed to make difference. It all began in 1993-1994. It was the time for change. It was the time that Northern Ireland brokered peace and the IRA and the Unionists bravely put their weapons beyond use. It was the time when Israel and Palestine called for a peaceful solution and the ordinary people in the world said no to war. It was the time that world leaders said 'Stop the Fighting'. It was the time that the United Nations made soldiers into Peace Keepers and a new incentive motivated nations to try to use negotiation not weapons to end conflicts.

There was new hope in the world and some dared to believe that we were entering into a brave new world, one where war was no more and where talking was indeed taking the place of bloodshed. I joined the United Nations Association and worked to collect items for the refugees in Bosnia. The man in the street took up the cause of the poor and the homeless and there was an energy and a knowledge that every person on the planet was connected to other persons on the planet, however far away and whatever their culture or race they mattered. Language was and is no barrier when a common cause and a common purpose arrests mankind, as it seemed to be doing then.

Since then, you and I have watched and seen the most amazing things happen in this century. Done by simple ordinary people who just wanted to find peace. We watched as the Berlin Wall came down, South Africa changed to a democracy, Clinton shook hands with Rabin and Arafat. Those involved in armed conflict in Ireland put weapons beyond use. I was with many a mere tiny encourager in a massive play on the stage of the world. On the sidelines I waited and prayed and wept for peace and I gave and gave anything and everything for peace and for God. I was sat alone with my candle and knowledge that Peace was and is Possible; we just have to start somewhere.

In my meditations and prayer I found that God was in His Nature, Truth, Love, Mercy and Peace. This nature began to affect mine and thus the first PeacePlease was written in an attempt to convey this to others. It was a book of poems about my experiences, which I sent to as many people I could. It is not quoted here because this book is designed to encourage you to be who you are and find your way to peace.

But – now- ten years on where are we? What has become of the peace that Israel aspired to, or the peace in the mind and hearts of ordinary people. I believe it is still there. It still hovers and flutters on what seems to be the brink of its annihilation whilst at the same time the nations wrangle and struggle to settle the world's problems with war.

But now here, I write about my beginnings. The beginning of my journey to find peace. I share this with you, so that it might add to your peace and maybe help you to make your own unique contribution to peace in the world. So that you become your own voice in the world joining all who hope for peace.

2. PeacePlease and Spirituality

What is Spirituality?

I believe it is all that is in us that connects us with the Spirit in the Universe that speaks of Love and Peace and wholeness. Have you ever gone out of your way to help someone when it was not in your best interests? I am sure you have. Did you feel good? That feeling is part of a connection within you that gives a feeling of rightness about actions. The feeling produces more love and compassion.

It is part of what connects you to the great Universal Spirit of Love and is part of that Truth, Mercy, Love and Peace we mentioned earlier. Have you ever seen a sunrise and felt that it is good to be alive? Have you ever thought of an idea that made you see more about the truth of a situation? These experiences are all part of you and your connection to what is called God.

I believe there is a Spirit in the Universe; I call it the Universal Spirit which is united to us and this Spirit of the Universe speaks within us in our thoughts, feelings and actions. It is within us and longs for our peace as much as we do. This is what I call God and is the essence of Truth, Mercy, Love and Peace.

Thinking then, of all the little things in life that make us have a feeling like that. Maybe it is a sunrise or a compassionate act. I wonder how many experiences like these we have that go unnoticed. Did you laugh with someone who was joyful, did you greet someone that you were pleased to see, and did they feel that pleasure? Did it make them feel good? Did you help an animal in distress and feel compassion? Have you ever given a child a drink of water? Have you ever helped an Old lady across the road or given up your seat on a bus for someone who was needing it more than you? All these feelings are part of the Great Spirit of the Universe within you. It is so big that it can be so little!'

Selfishness

Richard Dawkins in a TV interview said that he did not believe that there was such a thing as altruism. Altruism implies that there is no gain to the giver. In his book 'The Selfish Gene' he postulated that 'Survival of the species is the overriding mechanism by which we live.' We cannot be anything but selfish - can we? I loved that book but when I think of the word altruism, asking the question, 'Can we be altruistic?' feels like it is the wrong question. As Richard Dawkins says it is part of our nature to give to others in order to enable the species to survive. It is part of our nature, so we feel good about doing; it enhances the likelihood of survival. Feeling good is both biological and psychological. Built in goodness. There is in one sense no such thing as being selfish. But does that make it any less wonderful that it is built in.

There are choices that people make that are no doubt heroic and self sacrificing. The hero who rescues someone from the sea putting his own life at risk. Could this built in mechanism be something God gave us. Is this part of his plan, God's image in us? Is this why babies do not thrive without love or why our bodies react negatively to anxiety and anger and other negative emotions by producing harmful chemicals?

Many people spend their lives trying to understand whether their motives are pure and unselfish. They question whether they are doing something for themselves or for someone else and if they do not think they are pure enough in their motives, they do nothing. They guard their own spirituality. I say do it anyway? Throw away the guard and do what feels natural to do. Perhaps the following may help.

Truth, Mercy, Love and Peace. This is what I found God to be, the essence of TMLP. It is a good measure because you can say that as long as what I want to do is in line with the ideas of TMLP. I am in line with God and cannot do harm. I put it here because to begin with you may need a guideline to distinguish what is spiritual and what is not. This is my experience, that whatever is TMLP is God or in other words -Spirit.

The Truth of the situation will guard you from being manipulated. To do what is right does not mean you have to be a walk over, or that you cannot be creative or do things that will benefit you.. The Mercy will give you a perspective that looks for the good of the other and not just your own. Love will be in you and you will see the situation as it is and find a solution. Peace you will have and your mind will not be clouded in judgment so often and you will see what will make peace in a situation. It is only a guide and you will in time find your own.

So, for example, supposing you are in a situation where you are being bullied. It Maybe that you will meditate and find the following solution.

Truth will guard you from making false assumptions and clear your mind about exactly what is happening. What is the behaviour of the other person ? Without assigning emotion or what is he saying? Is it bullying at all. You might write it down:

1. He shouts at me (is he deaf?)
2. He says nasty things about me (does what he says mean that?)

Mercy would give the other person a chance and then get authoritative help if necessary.

Love will wish no harm so you will not look for revenge. Peace you will have through being merciful, truthful and compassionate.

Communication with God

Some would say to me - 'Do you really expect this Spirit of the Universe to communicate with you '? I will say, 'Yes'. The Nature of this Spirit I have found to be TMLP. It is that Love that flows between each of us and enlivens us. I did have a wonderful experience. I do not know how many people have them. I believe anyone can. I have never worried about guilt since the experience became part of my identity. When I have been concerned about anything I have talked to God in my prayers and waited for an answer. On occasions the sense of God and the feeling that he loves me keeps me steady. I do not have to exert any effort, the effort was and is not mine but God's. Forgiveness can only be felt by knowing that God has answered you in some way. Not necessarily through direct experience, sometimes these feelings resolve through meditation.

However you can interact with God. By practising meditation daily you can come to know the Spirit of God within your feelings and in your mind. Don't settle for anything else. Forgiveness and mercy IS extended to you. This can happen on your own or in a group or anywhere.

Of course you can relieve your conscience by going to religious leaders or those experienced at relieving guilt but you don't have to. If you need help, that is fine. Supposing that you don't find the freedom from guilt you look for but you don't need help, leave it and come back to it. You will get an answer.

Being and Finding Spirit

Find a space somewhere, sometime in your day. Even if you have 6 kids, three dogs and a few budgerigars it is still possible to find some time for you, to switch off, even if it is only for a few minutes. Make a conscious effort to make a time every day that is your time. Find a comfortable place to sit or rest and open your mind to the possibility that you are spiritual and that you are loved by the spirit of the Universe. Sit or rest, emptying your mind of everything. If you cannot do this easily, then work out what the problem is. Is it a rushing anxious thought? Or is it a worry about this process, if the latter read on and come back to it. What we are doing is being still. Perhaps you can say with me in your mind, I am a person; I am being still in my mind and in my body.

I am waiting quietly without any sense of rush or urgency, just waiting on the Great Spirit to be with me. I have no need to do anything in my mind or thoughts; I have no need to worry about what happens or does not happen for me in this few moments. It is not all my responsibility, it is up to the Spirit as well and I will know when I feel it, because those parts of myself that are already spiritual, that are influenced by TMLP will be uppermost in my mind. You may feel nothing and that is O.K too. I am still patiently waiting, patiently being, with no cause for alarm or trouble, for this is my still time. I am just being. So, I will be still, I will be quiet and I will be one with the Universe. If my thoughts do rush, I may contemplate a flower or a candle, the ancient and always new symbol of light and truth. I contemplate it without any effort of mine, without any need to be anything or think anything, great or small; I am just me sitting in a quiet and still place.

In stillness I am and in Stillness I be,
Until I feel the stirrings of the Spirit in me.
I'll know it and feel it as light and as peace,

As Love and compassion and mercy and truth,
I am still and am stillness completely at one
With the Great Universal
Who's known as just ONE.

The thoughts and feelings evoked by meditation are
evoked because God exists.

Great Universal Spirit of Love

The effect of your contemplation on your inner space
(awareness of yourself) will be unique to you. No two
persons are the same, they are all unique. You are unique.
There is no one else like you in the universe. No other
person has your mixture of genes or your background.
This is so important to realize that the Great Spirit is
interested in YOU as a unique person.

Think, please, of some way that your contemplation
has effected or enhanced your uniqueness and dwell on
that for a while. Above all you can be yourself, in the
truth of you. That means that you do not have to live
up to anyone else, behave in any special way, you only
have to be truly yourself. And, if you do not know who
you are, then dwell in that unknowing, that will be the
truth for you now. It is the Truth of that liberates and
does not condemn.

I have found that most people are afraid of themselves.
They expect to find that they are bad. Whatever you
feel about yourself this is for you. Even those who, on
the face of it look like the most hardened criminal has
goodness within. Often they have had the cruellest life

and have learnt to defend themselves and other family members. It is often this need for protection and to protect, that encourages violence in the person that has known nothing but violence.

Yet at the core of a person there is often love and kindness and heroic bravery. So, whatever YOU have DONE, OR FEAR, PeacePlease is for you. Maybe that is not your problem, maybe you are afraid of being good. Don't be afraid of your goodness, in the end it might suit you, OR, condemn yourself because you do not feel you have any. You may be so impoverished of love you feel nothing, that is OK you start where you are.

You may want to speak to the Great Spirit that is really fine, you will be answered. If you get thoughts that you have not known before, then let them be. If they are peaceful and loving then they are in the Spirit. If not discard them. If you find you cannot deal with them turn them over to the Spirit, just keep turning away from them and handing them to God. Sit with them, neither rejecting them nor harbouring them, always leaving them for a while. You might like to try this daily for quite a few weeks and of course if you feel you need help then of course, seek it. However, I have found that perseverance in this, will in the end give peace. There are no thoughts that cannot be left or transformed by contemplation. The answer is always to love. I found in the end after years of contemplation that those thoughts, feelings and actions that lead to love, peace and harmony are of the Spirit of Love. I found that there was indeed nothing that I could not resolve in this time of contemplation. You might find five minutes a day gets longer and longer, that is fine too. The Spirit can come to you, heal you and give you peace at any time.

Sometimes if nothing seems to happen immediately you feel impatient. That is because in our modern world we are used to making snap decisions and the need is for immediacy. If you cannot wait do the best you can.

The concept of guidance by God is largely one that belongs to the those that are used to 'God Talk'. Being guided by God in the modern world would probably be seen today as a psychiatric problem although there are more and more people drawn to eastern mysticism which is about 'communication' with God'. I prefer to see it as being in a state of unity between myself and the spiritual. If you wanted a sense of direct guidance about what God wants the following might help.

How do you discern the right direction among the myriads of thoughts and feeling that make up our lives? I think spirituality is more about a state of mind than a direction, although the state often means some things are excluded like lying or violence. But for the times you have to make a decision and you don't know what to do this might help.

Think of the situation. Then think of what you want. Imagine going towards one solution and then going towards the other. Does one feel more in line with your values than the other? Go with that. To find unity is to become more like your values.

If you imagine a light within you – the Spirit in you - it is at first quite small. As contemplation grows and the way you think becomes in line with TMLP the inner core grows. The thoughts, feelings and actions that are us and are from our being in unity with the Spirit grows and other thoughts and feelings become less. Your character is transformed into being more like TMLP and you learn what is right for you. Your heart leads you.

In a book I read on Christian, Jewish and Muslim mysticism the author talks about us becoming 'as gods'. We become so united to all that is God in us that we are able to react in that way. The Sufi who sits and contemplates becomes peace. The child who learns and loves the universe becomes joy. The ruler who learns about himself and all aspects of human nature becomes mercy. But at first you have to tune in. You do this by your meditation. As you meditate the truth comes to you also and this is the clarity and the Spirit. You can have a sense of deep peace and see situations differently. Go with it out of contemplation in little ways and test it for yourself. You will find that the truth that is revealed is also part of your personality.

Go with anything that moves towards love and peace in you. You may find you have an intense desire to seek the Spirit more, go with that but keep your circumstances in mind, you need to be very certain that any sense of giving is rational and within your means. Is it appropriate for your situation as well as anyone you feel moved to help. You have to sustain yourself financially. Trying to live in tune with the Spirit, moment by moment is demanding at first. The elements of what I found to be 'Spirit' were expressions of TMLP in me. Such values are never critical or harsh and never had the ring of binding conformity. It is almost better not to try but to practise contemplation and let things happen naturally.

You may notice things in your own life that you want to change. You may begin to find that you have new VALUES and that there are things that you care about that that you want to express. You may feel particularly concerned for peace, poverty injustice, you may find within yourself a desire to move towards peaceful and compassionate action.

The Psychology of PeacePlease may help you to conform your life to YOUR VALUES. Living according to your own values will automatically give you a sense of peace. Try it out and go with it. Check out what you discover if you are unsure. If you feel you want to give up your job and go and look after refugees, check it out. What do you need, is it possible in your situation. If one day you are meditating and you find your self thinking of bad things. Get up and do something else and bring it back into your meditation with your candle or light. Do not go on any impulse that will hurt or destroy you or any other being whether human or animal. This way you stay safe. God can bare your uncertainty. So if you don't know don't do!

3. PeacePlease and Psychology

Once you have practised these meditations you will find changes within yourself. The real psychology is not about what effects religion has on society, or on how many people benefit from prayer, it is about what happens in your relationship to the Love of the Universe and understanding the nature of that relationship.

Living Spirituality.

Supposing you are now able to be peaceful, you feel a sense of peace and a sense of love. If there is something that troubles you, now, you are still in your mind. Bring into this sense of stillness the person or situation that troubles you. Stay there for a while. Then think –'What do they need and what do I need'. You will find some ideas come into your mind. You will know when you have finished the state of stillness because you will become more aware of everyday things and be ready for action. Do this often, returning continually to that sense of peace and love.

It may be that you will see immediately what to do; it may be that you will feel that you should wait for a while. Is it a situation or person? Can you resolve it or do you need help? If you have an idea of what to do, think about it when you are out of the state of meditation and if it still seems OK to you even, if it is outside your normal pattern of what you do, act on it. Only by acting on it will you know whether you can trust this part of you that will guide you in everything.

When the intuition is right you will know and there will be a sense of calm and clarity, you will have an inner conviction about what to do. This is safe. It may be you are in a conflict with someone else; you may need a mediator or another organisation to help. Or, you may find your attitude changes.

I have never found this process of meditation to lead me outside of the law. If what you feel leads to anger or violence or discord leave it and bring those feelings and thoughts of discord into the same process. Do not act in anger; you cannot be clear about solutions. Anger causes a loss of perspective and you see things only from your own point of view. Gradually you will see what you need to do about you too. What inner process do you need help with; find a helper if you need it, there is no shame in it. Return again to that sense of peace thinking of the great Universal Spirit of Love and Peace. The lack of discord within oneself often leads to discord with others. If one can maintain a sense of peace and stillness then one will not necessarily be the instigator of discord elsewhere but one cannot guarantee that. As I have said before being peaceful does not seem to necessarily to either bring one into contact with like minded people, or bring about a situation of peace around one. Sometimes it is the opposite but you can be peaceful just about anywhere. If you are peaceful within yourself then you can cope with whatever you have to face. Living spiritually is to live according to your own understanding of the truth. the truth about you, the truth about others and the truth about the way things should be. You will then be at peace. You will also live in Love for others with your own Love and you will be merciful in whatever way you find it is in you to be. You will need no guru or priest the Kingdom of God will be within you. This is OK because you can only live YOU.

Universal respect.

In this relationship with the spirit you learn about you. Mostly you find the positive part of you and this is often more difficult to bear than any negative thing you may discover. Accepting that you can be all the good things you aspire to be can be a shock. It puts you into a different relationship with the Great Universal Spirit, you think differently about yourself and others. It affects those around you in ways you have no direct knowledge of. You go with this Spirit and you are changed forever. You go with this Spirit and heaven only knows where you might end up. As we have said in the last chapter everyone deserves your respect. Even your enemies are human beings and created and wonderfully scientifically engineered beings. They too are the temple or housing for the amazing spirit of love and peace, even if they do not see it. Even if you don't see it!

In many ways the start of this was an abnormal situation. I had parted company with the church, I was very poor, and I had thrown myself into my relationship with God. Could one rely totally on God, could one find God in such a way that you did only what God said. And, if you did what would happen. That was the beginning and I did it and it is true you can. But is demanding and appears risky. In many religions risk taking and devotion are seen as synonymous. My experience was that any risk was not planned and it is not a necessity to be close to God.

As I have described it before I lived in a way that made me feel that I experienced Jesus closer than breathing. In this state one knows little but Love and ones' compassion just is. That means that unless one has conviction and compassion that taking a risk is the right thing to do -don't. One knows that the action is right because you are only aware of love and the need of the other person. That doesn't mean one should never say no. Sometimes manipulators seeking to take advantage of generosity; will take and not necessarily use what they take in the right way. You are not meant to be used by all and sundry.

The other situation that often occurs where an action might be described as risk taking is when your integrity or what you believe is threatened. If you try and live peacefully then what seems to happen is, that anyone and everyone will do their best to stop you, seemingly in your best interests. You can be faced with a dilemma, live by conscience or by the dictate of others. I have never found it to be wrong to live by what I feel to be right. There are times when my circumstances make me question what I believe but I am determined to live this way to the best of my ability, even if I fail sometimes I get up and start again. For example, you might want promotion at work, living this way means that you do nothing to hurt another person to get it. In the 'rat race' others are not so considerate and then if you want to be at peace you must stand your ground. Meditation will help even if you do not think it will. If you have come to a point where you recognize the dilemma then it has already worked. In trying to live in a state of peace, mercy, truth and love you leave yourself open to others trying to meet their own unmet needs through you, in ways that appear as manipulation and which you need to resist. It is not always helpful to meet other people's needs in the way they appear to want. For example if someone needs accommodation is it helpful to give money to that person? It may be, but it may be they need to find their own way to independence. When others try to take advantage of me I ask the question, 'What is in this person's best interest'? Secondly I might ask, 'What do I need or want, is it possible that the two can be met at the same time?' I have a choice too, and I need to look after myself too. It is a delicate balance that only you can decide on.

Relationship.

You have to find out about you and about you and God and the only way you can do that is by meditation and carrying through your conviction.

After doing the earlier chapters you may be beginning to find out about you, what you believe in and what you feel is right for you to do.

In order to have a real psychology of a relationship with the Great Universal Spirit of Love, you have to be in relationship to it. The easiest way is with the above methods. What I found was that as I turned to God, I entered a relationship. to this 'God'. You could describe it as a relationship to that which is within me that is aligned to God. This strengthened me and became my wisdom. No one else should interfere with this. You can only live your own spiritual journey. You may be with someone on a spiritual journey but you cannot take it over or it will cease to exist.

To me and many like me God became my significant 'OTHER'. The being in my life I relate to. This should in my opinion be what spirituality is about and research into religious experience needs to look at this aspect of relationship with God or it is just touching the surface. Psychology in this context has not even begun to research this deep and difficult area. Some attempts have been made to understand cultures which include religion. Most research has showed that prayer and mediation can aid recovery from illness, have an effect on pain, heal illnesses and provide a more positive view of life. However, this still misses out the vital ingredient that I call the X factor. That is God himself. There has to be a two way interaction and this should be the stuff of research.

Anger and Aggression.

Another area that is important in finding peace and which has been extensively researched is the area of aggression.

Understanding what anger and aggression are, is important in peace psychology. It is also important for each person to understand their own difficulties in this area. Aggression and anger come from a sense of threat. Research shows we can be angry because of threat to territory, belongings, relationships, beliefs, values, position in society and self esteem. If you experience anger you are probably threatened by one of these. However, habitual anger can lead to an attitude which gives repetitive free rein to anger and this is called aggression. The end result of this is often hostility and a state of mind that is given to angry and aggressive thoughts much of the time. But here let us think about the psychology of each one of the above threats, as the purpose of this writing is to give insight and this will serve this purpose well.

Threat to territory and property/possessions.

To loose precious things if very hard to deal with and there is so much suffering over these situations. Firstly, I want to give you my spiritual perspective which may at first seem hard to understand. The perspective is that in one never really owns anything that is material. Barker the philosopher said we really only know things through our sense perceptions. We touch a table and we feel it is there. We see a sunset and our senses tell us there is a sun. Without the touching and without the seeing we would not know of the table or the sun. You could argue then that ownership is not then necessary. However, what ownership gives one in the material sense is the right to have a boundary around the said territory or object and to control what happens to it and to you. It is if you like a battle about control of actions of others not about ownership per se. The reason for saying this is because there is a lot of self esteem and value attached to getting things and I want to say that that isn't absolutely necessary for a person's self worth. I give and example from my own experience.

I had left the church dispossessed. I had left my career to follow a call and as usual it was all or nothing for me. I had in any case abandoned myself to God. Now here I was no job, no priesthood, poor and mocked, sitting in my Jesus sandals at a service I was supposed to have trained to do. I had nothing at all. A few books and odds and ends. I had written to everyone I could think of about my vision for peace. I was hopelessly in love with God and Jesus. At that that moment visions and joy seemed to become like nothing - what the hell was I doing?

Then the hymn took off. It was a glorious warm sunny day. The sea sparkled. The air was fresh and warm. 'Morning has broken like the first morning; blackbird has spoken like the first day'. Then...mine is the sunlight, mine is the morning, mine is --- I realised -------in that moment of time that even though I had nothing, I had everything. Barker was right, we own our sense perceptions of what is before us but we do not really own anything. When we close our eyes the table is not ours. Close you eyes and the house is not there. Touch the table and it is there?

Suddenly life was a whole lot better. I no longer needed to own anything. Standing in the dole queue wasn't so bad! I walked along the sea front and I owned the sea! I walked through stately homes and gardens and for as long as I was there and for as as I remembered it, it was mine. For me ownership is now a question of control. That is for me what territorial arguments are about. The right to control what happens on a piece of land or to an object. There is no real ownership. After that joy filled my days and ever since wherever I am and whatever state I am in there is always something that fills my senses with joy. Detached from everything, I own everything. Is that then all there is to it?

Well yes and no, because if you have no rights, life can be very miserable. I own very little and there are times I need to own the rights to space, silence and the room to be. In worn torn lands the people need the right to be who THEY are without hindrance and without prejudice.

So how do we solve the real problems which involve threat. What about war ? Is it so silly to think about talking!

There is a wonderful book called, 'Non-violent Communication-The language of compassion.' By Rosenburg. It deals with a way of finding solutions to warring factions by trying to meet the need. It is basis for conflict negotiation and is simply put: 1. What is your need? 2. What is my need? 3. Can we meet in the middle? 4. Can we agree? If we agree we have a WIN WIN solution. That is, everyone gets something they want or need. Much negotiation goes on within this sphere. Sometimes if there is not agreement it is better to stay separate until there is one. OR, if the threat is too great then one must remain on waiting, to find the solutions. I believe that there is a solution to every dilemma but it requires patience on all sides to find it. War is not the real answer.

I find this works in my daily life when there are the usual difficulties and problems. Often one has to bide one's time until all parties are able to negotiate. Ireland is a magnificent example of this as brokered peace learched from one crisis to another.

Threat to relationships.

In every day life as well as on the international scene, relationships are vital, important and what we are involved in, whether we like it or not. One of the causes of conflict is jealousy.

Morbid jealousy is a condition that exists in the field of psychology and it refers to the feelings and thoughts associated with jealousy. Mostly we are taught to think of jealousy as a green eyed monster. However, this is really the opposite of what it is, although the effects can ruin and devastate lives.

Jealousy happens when one thinks one is too little or insignificant. When you think that what someone else has, or is, is necessary to your well being, even sometimes to life itself. Wanting what someone else has puts one in a one down position if you don't have it. To deal with it you have to question the root cause of the jealousy. Is the problem the over valuing of something or someone. Often I hear of suicides because someone has lost someone or they have been the looser in a love triad. Then the individual involved does not see their own life as important or valuable without the desired companion. Then it is time to see the problem for what it is and get help if need be. I believe something like this goes on in the stuff that starts wars. The relationships that are formed in societies become under threat. Sometimes the 'the thing' one wants, grips us and takes control. This I believe is what Jesus meant when he said that 'one can gain the whole world and loose one's own soul'. Our soul, the person we are, is so possessed that we are not able to stay in control without it. Our individual freedom, our own volition and independent decision making is lost to the object of our desire. We are imprisoned by the 'thing'. Buddhism has a similar idea about the need for detachment. Barker is the solution again. It is what we believe about our value. From a Peace Please perspective the Truth would be that every unique person is a child of the Universe and infinitely valuable. Mercy would free the person from jealousy and Love would help for the sufferer to see their true value.

Beliefs and Values.

Beliefs and values are the unconscious rules we live by, that we have built up over time, probably since early child hood. When these are thwarted we are angry especially if they are dearly held beliefs about what we need. For example: 1.I believe I should be treated well. 2. I believe I am being treated badly. These beliefs if thwarted will threaten our self esteem and make us angry.

A fair and just society is our right.

If we see something that does not tally with these beliefs we become angry... The Answer however is to hold all these things lightly. Having a sense of light attachment, knowing ourselves to be, as human beings, infinitely more valuable than anything. Meditation can help with this by becoming clearer about who we are and how valuable we are to God and to others.

This is a difficult concept to grasp. Most people do not believe in themselves. Neither do they believe in the goodness of their fellow human beings. Doubt and suspicion lurk because for the most part people make assumptions about others without checking out the facts. What others say can therefore influence careers, families, position in society etc. I have found the only way of dealing with malicious sleaze is to psychologically detach from it. Because I know who I am,

I know that often the thing said is untrue or distorted. One cannot in the main control what others think or what they say, it is therefore of little value to deal with it because one then gets drawn into an argument and that gives more weight to the distorted truth. Of course if there is a clear argument, that is different but gossip and the like will grow with challenges unless you have enough clear evidence to go to court. Usually those who distort the truth are not interested in knowing the facts. Replies fuel further distortions. The only thing I can do is live as I am and not worry about other peoples opinions except to use the law appropriately if the situation impinges too much. One then has to look at why position matters. Does it matter to get something done or is it a need for recognition, in which case the need must be met in some way. One has to value oneself as one is and find the niche you are meant to be in. Again meditation can help.

Self Esteem.

The term 'self esteem' is a psychological concept which measures the degree to which you view yourself positively. How much do you think of yourself? We are given our self esteem as children by our parents. They give us a sense of being valuable. Many of the people I see have never felt valued by anyone. They often have never felt safe or loved or wanted. They may travel through their lives always feeling that way, unless they meet others who value them or they find some way that they value themselves. Sometimes they seek others attention inappropriately to find a sense of 'child worth'. Then the only answer is to find it in yourself or you become prey to those who take advantage and manipulate. If your self esteem is built around how successful you are then that is fragile. If success fades then what is left are shattered dreams.

This perspective says that there is respect and love for all, finding that you are valued by The Great Universal Spirit of Love. That there can be another way of finding that part of you that is part of God. This leads to being valued and being the real you and it does bring a sense of positive regard for yourself. There is always something about your self that you can regard as positive as you find that this Great Universal spirit of Love values YOU.

Position in Society

Your position in society that is your relationships to other people in your community is very important. In many ways whatever we do or don't' do will effect our relationships and our self esteem.

I believe that some positions are time limited. Then, the question is whether the role can be adapted to something else, or it may be new direction is called for. Hanging onto a long forgotten ideas leads to frustration for everyone. Positions and ideas have there day and are always superseded by new ones. However, if you are unjustly thrown out of a job and loose one's home, family and position in society then anger is inevitable.

When this happens taking a step back from the situation and viewing the situation A film on an imaginary screen in your head may help you to see objectively what has happened. Then you will be able to see what to do. For example someone is sacked for standing up for another worker's rights. He looses his income his home and his family. He is left homeless and stateless. Firstly it is a good idea to get over the pain of the betrayal and take action through legal means. It is then important to see that the other person had their problems. Maybe they were being threatened. This looking at the situation from the other person's point of view is what takes the bite out of anger. We see the other person as someone like us, who is as vulnerable and weak as we are. We cannot continue with aggression if we truly see this. Once this resolution is reached it is time to 'move on'. Take up a new position and put past experience into good use. This might be by joining a union for example, or taking up apposition to make sure that other people do not suffer in the same way. This brings positive out of disaster.

4. PeacePlease: You and Your Community

By now you may have some idea of what is important to you. What of all the values beliefs and thoughts that go through your mind are the ones that inspire YOU. These are not thoughts that inspire me, or anyone else. The essence of PP is not that you follow me or any person but that you find what it is within yourself that inspires you to act. What I want is for everyone who cares to do so, to find their own spirituality and their own truth. Otherwise the strength and the power that lies within each person lies dormant and a rather distorted view of a copy is all that is achieved. How to do this and remain within your own truth in society is the question that I hope to answer in some small way in this chapter.

So beginning again from the start of this part of PP I would like to ask a question: What do you think is important about society? What is important about that? What do you do on a day to day basis that you think is important? For example you may be a teacher who has entering the profession because you feel that you have something to offer those who are struggling to learn, or, you may be interested and think that disadvantaged children should be given help. Or maybe you are interested in the academic side of learning. These thoughts and desires are essential to your spirituality. Some of the thoughts and feelings that I found emerging from my own peaceful meditation were peace, the plight of those caught up in war. The problems of the infrastructures following war and the poverty that followed. Poverty, especially the problems in South Africa and the needs of the third world to find a respectful and hopeful way of life, were problems that entered my thoughts in meditation. I also expressed my values by being involved with the problems of neighbourhoods that are in conflict and by helping soldiers who suffered from Post Traumatic Stress Disorder. For all of these values I found, ways of making some contribution. I joined the United Nations Associations and watched hours of TV footage on foreign affairs. I became a mediator for the Neighbourhood Dispute Service and made collections for refugees. I became united within myself. I felt I was, what I was always meant to be. My own community values expressed in what I did in the community. This is part of unity.

5. PeacePlease and Society

It would seem impossible for us to think of a society of people that would and could be peaceful. Heaven on earth? How would it be if everyone co-existed in a way that met their needs and everyone else's? It can be done, because it is done, in many ways.

The only way, is by each of us looking into our own hearts and finding a way to live it for ourselves. One way of thinking about it, is to think about how that might look in our institutions in our society.

Education.

Education was one of the first institutions to be run for everyone equally and to a large extend follows values such as TMLP. Education. was seen as paramount in the UN mandate Agenda for Peace In 1995. The first education packs were published and model general assemblies and security councils called MUNGAS were formed, giving young people a chance to role play real international situations and to contribute to the United Nations Association. (UNA). The UNA is a volunteer non- governmental organisation which provides forums for discussion and a watch dog activity for the UN.

Many other enterprising movements in Education inspire us. The cross border Schools and workshops in Northern Ireland for example provides opportunities to break down the barriers between religious groups. Peer mediation at the end of the nineties gave young people a way of learning to sort out their own differences without resorting to violence. The opportunities for young people to take up a mantle for peace are endless. If bullying could be eradicated this would be a tremendous victory for peace. Often children learn to be aggressive in the playground. TMLP is in evidence everywhere. Children are given second chances, they are taught to tell the truth and to give to others and there is a movement for children to become mediators rather than fighters. Thousands of pounds are lost by sickness, suicides and lack of achievement in the work place because of bullying. Can we have an anti bullying surge, I wonder?

Health.

Maybe you are a doctor or a nurse or a domiciliary in the health care system. Most people who enter health care do so out of a sense of wanting to help others. Often what they find is that the system mitigates against real help because of the lack of resources. We need and I include myself as a health professional, to be reminded that the individual has needs and values which need to be heard and care, needs to be needs led. Again the stance of deep respect and care is paramount. Often sickness comes from disunity within the person when their values and beliefs and potential is not fulfilled. In the main I think that the health service does an amazing job. The sticking points are the lack of resources and energy and at the moment the need to 'be seen' to care rather than actually fostering a caring community of health workers. This is not because individual workers don't care but because the time and energy spent, particularly in the mental health field, does not match the need. Whatever your level of professionalism the values of TLMP can apply in the following way: Truth in every aspect of society would mean that that we could trust each other. Telling the truth is not a popular concept but it does work. If everyone lies how can we really communicate? No one would ever know if what they think they know, actually is!

Law

Justice is established truth.

This statement is a statement which is complete in itself. That is that for justice to 'be', the truth of a situation it must be reliably revealed in the conclusion of a situation of injustice. Here the wrong is righted. For example someone A, steals something that we know belongs to someone else called B. The truth is that what A has, should be in the possession of B. Establishing truth would be that the item stolen would be returned to A by B. This would be justice in truth. Truth in relation to justice is an interesting idea. John Rawls saw Justice and Truth as being superior in effect than compassion. He said that Justice has no need for compassion.

If we take TLMP as something that can exist and be reflected in our great institutions would John Rawls be right? Would it be possible to have a 'Justice' that included, Truth, Love, Mercy and Peace. We know that in many ways the law is about the 'truth' of a situation But if we think for a moment of criminal law how would this co-exist with the idea of retribution. I'm not sure that it does, as long as retributional justice is the only ingredient in the outcome. Many offenders have social backgrounds of deprivation. If justice were to operate here in terms of truth that would also need to be accounted for and worked on At the present time there does not seem to be enough resources to care or do anything about the causes of crime in terms of individual need.

Unlike John Rawls, I believe that justice can be a derivative of compassion. Justice and retribution cannot be a final state in a case, or there would be no room for change. One of the logical fallacies of the death penalty is that there is no room for change.

If Truth is established, as above, Love would see the point of view of the offender; Mercy would see the mitigating circumstances and look for the reason behind the offence. Peace would be the resolution that is justice for both parties. The victim would be granted a restoration of the original state he or she was in before the crime. Love would see that compensation must be made, and the Truth would be restored. The offender may make amends to the victims, thus seeing his customer as human.

In situations of aggression when offenders react to others out of threat, for example, and who see others as threatening because of a violent childhood, retributional justice will make things worse. The offender from this kind of background needs to experience something different, the outcome must include a way of putting right the plight and the distress of the offender. This would be a PeacePlease solution.

I believe that our justice system is amazing and the backbone of our society. There Is much TLMP in all of it. But we need more. Supposing that an offender is truly sorry and has made amends, that is he has tried to put right his crime. Is punishment which is supposed to help the perpetrator to reflect on their misdeeds really going to help? Would it not be better to foster and encourage the direction in which reparation is made rather than put that often young person in the harsh and difficult environment of prison?

Retribution is a military term which states that that the punishment for the crime should equal the suffering caused. However it may not take into consideration the cause of the problem. If it were to do so, then one would have to understand the psychology of the case. I have never met anyone in my time as a psychologist who had offended that didn't have a problem. It is a well known and widely held opinion in clinical forensic psychology that the solution to the crime is often not prison and retribution but is often education and sometimes treatment.

Punishment and reward as a system can only work if the person's psychological perspective is taken into account. Other wise it becomes a role play. Research shows that reward has to be a vital ingredient for it to work. For Justice to be truth it needs to account for the victim and the perpetrator. In order for society to be just, there must be the micro and the macro perspective. The macro being the effect on whole collective of people and the micro the individual. If the latter is sorted the former must follow.

Distributive justice

It would follow then, that the distribution of justice would extend to everyone From macro to micro and from micro to macro. That would be for wealth, education, health and all of society's givens. As far as wealth goes there would have to be a balance whereby the labourers who create wealth for business owners have some say and proportion of the profits. Also ownership of one's work is seen as a positive aspect of healthy employment by organisational psychologists. That would mean that the credit for a job well done went to the person who did it.

Institutions would reflect justice. Justice can then be divided into two broad perspectives:

1. The definition of just behaviour and concern for genuine respect and treatment which is to be regarded as fair and equal for all.

2. The administration of the law which ordains legislation imposed by a judge or magistrate of a supreme court to a country or state, with objectives that uphold the above and protect the victims and pursue the perpetrators lawfully. This might also include 'provision for the meeting of the real needs of the offender'. Which

might mean prison but would more likely mean education and social reintegration.

Plato said that if you have a JUST PERSON you must have a JUST CITY STATE. Justice is the proper harmonious relationship between the warring parts of the person or city. If we applied the above we might then have TMLP within our system, as part of the law applied.

6. PeacePlease and Religion

Firstly, I am no expert on world religions and this chapter is not meant to offend anyone. This is my perspective alone and is not the result of any religious input. I write because I believe what I am writing.

I believe religion was made to help man to God and not for man to serve religion. What matters is to find the peace and a relationship with the Spirit. If religion were to take its proper place in our lives we should be united with each other. War, based on religious difference happens because everyone thinks they have the exclusive truth about God.

It is possible to look on our fellow men as if through the eyes of the Compassionate Christ, with the mercy of the Merciful Allah, the wisdom of the Wise Buddha and with the respect of the Great One God and Lord of all. There are pointers in many of today's religions that peace and not war is to be most desired. The pillar of cloud in the Old Testament, The birth of Christ, the conversations in the Bhagavad Gita and the Truth, Mercy, Love and Peace of the One spirit over all.

To some I extent I think Marx was right. Religion is the opium of the people. It is the drug that maintains the status quo. It is the structure that keeps everyone singing the same song from one hymn sheet. The problem is that the hymn never changes. I believe religion is supposed to lead us to a relationship with the Great Universal Spirit of Love. The dynamic healing transforming power of love.

Spirituality can help us enter into such a relationship. Spirituality is different from religion, because it puts spirituality first. Spirituality should be the result of religion but often it yields only adherence to rules.

It doesn't t matter to me whether you have a religion or not, although this is for those that have none, you are welcome to read it if you do. I only ask that you leave the arguments about who is right and who is wrong elsewhere while you read.

From this perspective God is God, the Great Universal Spirit of Love. Those arguments do not belong here because following this perspective you can never be Completely right about God. He is the Great Spirit of the Universe, His mind created it and out of his thought we became. How then can we dictate to God who and what He can be and who and what any other person can or cannot believe? We can only seek to do what the Spirit shows us in our own lives and contribute to others when and if they will allow. We cannot judge them or kill them because they are not the same as us. We can only serve them and love them in the Spirit of the One God of the Universe. For, this is His goal - the Kingdom of God on earth. This Kingdom would be full of Truth, Mercy, Love and Peace and it is possible. It is possible if through spiritual and intellectual thought everyone becomes aligned to TMLP. Then I do not judge, The Lord, Allah or the Buddah. Neither to I judge

Judaism or Christianity or other faiths. Living TLMP I know and experience in myself God's kingdom. Then I become my own formula for peace.

Religions in the world.

I see religion as that which engages our thought processes, our emotions and commitment. If it is to aid us spiritually then the spiritual communion with the Spirit must come first. It must be that which we do. We watch the media, mainly through TV, seeing the colours and hearing the sounds which represent the core expressions of religious practise. Each religion having its own colour and sound, its own tradition of worship and its own doctrine and code of living. How then can any one say that it is possible for the religions of the world to behave as one? They can if they see themselves as individual, spiritual beings, united to the Great Universal Spirit of Love. They can if they let each other be what they are and accept that everyone is different.

I believe that unity between the Roman Catholic Church and the Anglican Church is only possible if the basis of this is spiritual union. Otherwise the whole argument becomes an exercise in who can produce the best possible wording for documentation that has to represent both traditions. Important though that is, I see spirituality as the sharing of prayer, the sacraments and the knowledge of the experience of God. The Koran, the Torah whichever spiritual writing you aspire to they can all speak to us of God.

From my own experience which was not because of any merit in me but God given I walked, lived and breathed Christ and His Spirit within. As I did so. I found that I was drawn to very unlikely places. Places that I was reluctant to go. However, the feelings I had within were those of a conviction to be with and a desire to be one with others, whilst at the same time experiencing intense pain at doing something that as a Christian one would ordinarily associate with sin, misplaced devotion, going against the Gospel, even going to hell. But still I was sure that the Christ within me was leading me to go to different religious houses. Part of me cried out with just about every text one could think of that would chide against such an action. But still I went in faith.

The first place I went to was a Buddhist meeting where the service comprised of chanting. I found to my surprise a deep sense of the abiding eternity of life - that is the best way I could describe it. I felt the chanting lifting me above all that was an influence to negativity and I came away positive and amazed that the Christ I loved and felt devoted to, wasn't particularly devoted to Himself - but rather He was and is Peace and Unity. His love transcended all boundaries. When I went to the synagogue I found a mystery of time, it was as if their songs echoed down through the eons of time and eternity itself, down to us sitting in the synagogue. When the scrolls were lifted from their resting place and the horn was sounded I had an incredible feeling of being part of something that had come to us through eons of time. Something that thousands, millions of worshipers has been part of before. It was awesome and solemn.

In the Mosque I found the fervour for the Gospel, or at least the sermons could have been evangelical any day. What amazed me was the similarity between Islam and Christian morality. I particularly took to reading the Koran and found a whole passage where the prophet Mohamed chides Christians for not being Christian enough. The insights I got from my contact with and reflection on Islam were that one, God had already provided a foolproof salvation and two, the nature of God as compassion was as real in Islam as it was in Christianity. From my perspective Christ did it all, for everyone, on the cross.

I read the Koran and still do, from the perspective of the west, trying to look through the eyes of Mohamed. What I imagined was, a Mohamed inspired but up against it. He, like St.Paul seemed to have a direct revelation which he gave to others as the way one should live.

Every time a revelation happens it seems to be in response to something that is happening to the people of that religion. It seems to be a contrast to something else. At the time of the experience, it always appears to the receiver to be vital, true and must be shared. It usually starts off a change in the community of believers and usually causes conflict with those who adhere to previous thought. The question is can religious thought adapt when the religion itself is convinced that the original truth is the only one. The difficulty is that most people are afraid of God and afraid that if they try something new they are disobeying God. That usually means some adverse consequence like hell or damnation and often means the individual is ex- communicated.

Actually, I believe that the nature of the experience itself is vital, all encompassing, the only truth to the person who is receiving it. If it wasn't you wouldn't do anything about it. I don't believe that it is always the last word of God. If it was God would be effectively dead with nothing else to say! This is where most Christians are.

Writings of mystics say the same, there is Universal Spirit of Love and the beholder sees themselves as precious to God and having something vital to say. Unfortunately this is never a happy state to be in if you are in the middle of an authoritarian style of religious expression. The very nature of the experience is bound to cause trouble!

I found that the awesomeness of the Great Universal Spirit of Love was not bound by any religion, in fact He seemed to be everywhere. In the pages of the Koran I found Him, in the pages of the Bible, The Torah and the Bhagavad-Gita. There was the love, often masked but there. I found this very awesome.

God is above it all.

I believe that this says it all for most religions. We all get caught up in the religion and keep trying to save God from His demise in the world, no matter what it costs, without the realization that as God He could do it all any day. Somehow though, He wants and needs us.

I have to say that one of the stages of spirituality that I went through was a process of identification with Christ which led to the stigmata. During this time I felt in Love with Christ and in a sense responsible for His demise in the world. I was to a degree in such an involvement that I felt compelled to make sure that every soul I met must know that Christ existed and that God loved them. Not only did I feel responsible for the delivery of His revelation to me and that -The World must stop fighting - I believed it completely and entirely.

What has become clearer to me over time is, however, that I can never make myself a judge over another or their religion. Or, be responsible for the salvation of others. I cannot be responsible for other's responses either. I had to grow into my experience and learn to trust its revelation, it to realise that God IS. God is for me the Great Universal Spirit of Love and He can do quite a lot for Himself!

If he wants land to go to another country, do we have to fight for it? Is that not more about the human side of us that tries to do what we feel God has said. Now I do what I think I should do and leave the rest. I urge those in the world who have conviction to claim land or anything else, to do what you can and leave the rest. Isn't life itself more important?

Are there not encouragements in the Torah, Koran and Bible to show kindness and mercy as a means of gaining divine favour? Is it not possible to do that instead of war and terror?

Religious Conflict.

The business of the truth is extremely difficult. Holy Books are seen as absolute Truth. I had a very enjoyable time with some Mormons, who came to see for about two months. We read the book of Mormon and we agreed and disagreed. We discussed and argued and prayed and drank coffee. The basics of having a belief in God were agreed but the crunch came when I knew that the next question for me was going to be ' Can you now see that the Book of Mormon is the only Truth'?

I said before asked, please do not ask - because it will divide us and end our friendship. By asking such a question you exclude any other truth and any future truth that might be revealed. The Living Word becomes that which is now dead. I cannot see the Living God in everyone else so I must exclude all others.

I believe the Holy Spirit (Spirit of God, Universal Spirit of Love, that which is in me that is like the Spirit) has Spoken to me through just about every religious Holy Book there is.

There are two issues here. One is that religious truth offered at the time of the revelation will meet the needs of the time and the person it is given to and this may be the kind of truth that always has a relevance. A bit like sayings like 'don't count your chickens before they hatch'. We all know what that means and so did our grandparents. But I don't think that what that means or what it might refer to will apply to us to use in the same way 300 years on, or that God vanished and died with the message. God is alive and wants to communicate with us all. Usually the message can be interpreted for any time but it adapts.

The second issue is the role of our humanity in the interpretation of revelation. I have often prayed for relief from harassment but never revenge. However, that is because of the vision that encourages love, mercy, truth and peace. I have been angry enough to pray against others but I don't. I pray for mercy. It is not far from my thoughts or yours that part of the vision is human. It comes through a human and therefore can never be infallible. With this is mind dare I or dare you pray for the harm of another? I won't!

So what of the truth? Do I accept my Mormon friend's words as true and does this mean they are the 'truth'? If I accept that what they say is true do I also have to sign up for 'all else' as exclusions? I opted for ' it's true but I cannot exclude others' and sadly we parted. But I still remember those evenings and their kindness.

Unfortunately, most religions require you to sign up for their truth and their truth alone and to exclude all else which is partly why I do not have a religion. This is in part to do with social togetherness. But it is also the core reason there are wars over religious rites, territory and beliefs when the religion is the cause and not the excuse. The second issue that: God is so alive and so much in life that He can speak to us through anything, even a donkey!

If we believe this and I do, it means that solutions do not only rest in the 'absolute' truth of the sacred text but one is free to find a solution based on the reality that God is Compassion, Mercy, Truth and Love. The Great Universal Spirit of Love helps us an attitude of non-judgmental compassion that invites us into the kingdom!

We then do not have to fight! You can have your truth that you have had through of time and look for a new way now to reconcile yourself to all those who are spiritual beings whatever their creed.

Unless we can see each other, whether Jewish, Muslim, Buddhist, or Hindu as equal to us, we cannot truly live in Peace and we put ourselves and our Holy Books above God Himself. That does not mean that you cannot be a really fantastic Catholic and abide by all the rules of the church, or you cannot be truly faithful Jew or devoted Muslim. God does reveal Himself through all these religions but I believe they are not the last word. God is. If we hold the creator of the Universe as first and religion as Second, then our perspective changes to one where religion is our aid and not our goal. If we can see our brothers and sisters of all religions as all having a truth about God that might be valuable to us, then we will not and cannot cause them pain. As Jesus said Sabbath was made for man and not man for the Sabbath. Religion is not an end in itself. God is.

Without letting go of religious loyalty there may be no possibility of religion becoming a unifying factor rather than a divisive one. The root of this conflict I believe is that of fear. It is not devotion itself but rather insecurity that somehow one will transgress against God. That is of course admirable in itself but it will not bring peace. One has to, in my opinion, give God some credit and let Him stand by His own Words, that He can deliver us from whatever afflicts us. Then laying down arms becomes not a matter of letting down our religion but of respecting our fellow human beings rights to be who they are AND having faith, letting God be bigger than we are in all our weakness.

I wonder if maturing in faith is also a sort of letting go, not of everything you believe in and treasure but of what one needs in terms of identity within a faith and reassurance of the truth. As one becomes more aware of God in everything, it is as if ones eyes are opened. So what I would say to those who dare not think that there is any truth outside of their own religious tradition, 'Does God leave you at the temple door, whichever door that is'? 'Is there any temple door that he is outside of'? It may be that we all need to go the extra mile in trying to understand other faiths. I was fervently devoted to Christ. It was as if the fervour had become so completely part of my being that I could let it rest somehow, assured that God was still very much God wherever I was. But it took some believing and some risk.

I am sure I was seen as a fanatic. After my experience of Christ I wanted nothing but to know more and experience more of the same. My mind was completely turned towards God and my mind and will completely captured by religious fervour. I could not conceive of any other religion being right. I do not think I was unbalanced. I was not psychiatrically ill and nor was I emotionally disturbed. I was sent by the church to see professionals who said that they could not explain my experiences but I was not psychiatrically ill. Yet, the absolute devotion I felt which was akin to being in love, completely threw me and those around me. They could not understand or relate to it. Fanatic! This term however, is derogatory. It does not explain what is happening to one on the inside. What was happening was my mind and my will were changing and my orientation was being turned towards God.

I had a very intense and close relationship with Him. The purpose of which was to draw me into a state of being bonded with God. If I was not so emotionally and mentally switched into God I doubt that the changes that occurred within me, would have occurred. It was to God I turned in my misery at being excluded and mocked. Every pain and hurt I turned over to God and it became transformed. That does not mean that mockery and rejection should have, or, should happen. Religion is too often the excuse for cruelty and even death. I don't believe that this right. I do not think sacrifice is right. I do not believe that Jihad means suicide bombing. I believe that caring for the poor and the sick isright. I believe that sacrifice occurs as a result of normal situations when one's integrity demands it. I do not think it can be demanded. There has to be a choice or it is co-ercion or even murder. I believe the Koran is beautiful, but I cannot go with needless killing. I believe the Bible beautiful but I do not believe God wants killing. I believe many religious books contain truths about God but I also believe they are written by humans and as such will always be partially human. .Haven't most prayed for deliverance from a person or situation. That doesn't have to be violence. I never pray for harm to another person and I believe that is right. I pray for God's will and MERCY.

The relationship I had with God was of a friend and parent. I did not go anywhere without sanctioning it with God. This was the end of my experiment with God. It was, I found, possible to live like the Starets (Pilgrims) of Russia. I found the most Amazing things happened I began to trust God and He became my sole source of comfort. As this journey continued the intensity of attachment was not longer needed and I Relaxed, more assured of God and of my security. I was healed of so much I cannot even begin to tell it here. Physically I was healed and mentally the scars of the past went. I was completely and absolutely at peace. Calm, serene and totally unified.

I truly believe that the fanaticism of religions may be something like the beginning of a healing process. It may also be the beginnings of a person being transformed by God. The derogatory label should go out of the text books and diagnostic criteria, it is not relevant. It is hurtful to those who are genuinely trying to make sense of a very delicate balance within themselves, that is, the God bit!

When whole religions become fanatical then I believe we should be stopping to listen to what they are fanatical about and give them room to go through the process. I do not mean that I sanction violence or anything that undermines or hurts another human being. This may not be religious fanaticism but political or social domination. You can tell the difference. The person who is religiously inspired puts God first, the person who is politically inspired put the politics first and there is nothing wrong with that. You just need to be clear which it is. I found the vital ingredient in my life, the X factor – God. For me this stands for God. So Let God be God,

Let you be you and

Let I be I and Let us live in harmony together.

7. PeacePlease and Politics

I believe our politicians do a marvellous job and live their own ideologies as best they can. I propose that this philosophy can work more in politics than anywhere else. Love, peace, truth and mercy can be at the root of our political systems.

Love because ultimately even though our structures both organisational and physical seem to often deny human need, it is the needs of others for which politics really exists Political ideology forces the world to see and help others. TMLP Interpreted within the political system means thinking of the other persons' need and the integration of the needy into society by the system.

Peace because ultimately the serenity of inward peace transforms perspective. By adopting it we automatically look for opportunities to make peace and not war. Patience must be the hallmark of peaceful politics.

Truth because communication suffers when no one knows what anyone else knows and what anyone else does. In this day and age it is understandable that there is a certain amount of secrecy about what any party or nation does. However, it does not in my opinion really work. We have come from a state where secrets were the prerogative of special situations or special forces. Now the truth at large seems to be the minority in society. Logically this cannot work. It's like that amusing conversation that goes something like this' 'Hello, there, Nice to see you, I saw you know who, you know where at that time of day, you know what I mean'.

We will breed insecurity and fear. Telling the truth means that you know you are and so does everyone else. I believe we need more transparency not more secrecy with due regard for proper privacy. If no one never knows the truth how can anyone make accurate decisions.

We also need an acceptance that mistakes are made. In the professional world mistakes are intolerable. However, we are human. We do not learn if we do not acknowledge our mistakes. As far as government goes I wonder that anything is ever right. With so many factors to consider it is impossible to control everything. The plight of the politician is to produce the perfect and the impossibly right solution always.

Mercy is an unpopular word. It denotes to most, weakness and naivety. One is encouraged to think that in this day and age the only way to be is tough and unforgiving. Again we deny our humanity. It is impossible always to get things right and it is hopeful to have mercy on those who don't. Mercy has to be balanced by self interest. Otherwise It calls for impossible sacrifice.

The Self Interest of Politics!

In the selfish gene Richard Dawkins proposes that there is no such thing as altruism and that the only reality is that of survival, which of its very nature seems altruistic but actually serves to provide the means for the genes to continue onwards into subsequent generations.

My question is, 'is there anything wrong with being selfish? I would say no, as long as you recognize it and evaluate it, if it affects other people. . For example, mostly, world politics struggles to provide for the people within a system that dictates that the 'party' stays in power. The survival of the party ensures that the policies believed in actually happen. In many ways the care of the nations is second to the survival of the political system. These systems hi-jack serving the people in order to serve the people..

Adam and Eve were banished from the garden in the story of the beginning of creation. Why? Because Eve had thought for herself and had not obeyed God. She ate the forbidden fruit. You cannot decide for yourself then, unless you become your own god. I believe the Adam and Eve story signifies the maturational process of human life. Eve made a decision and both she and her companion had the knowledge of good and evil. We have that. We can decide.

I believe the answer lies again in truthful realism. In politics one can say this or that is for the party. We need to do this or that for the people and keep control of the this or that for the party. Once realised it is very easy to decide if the decision can go ahead or not.

For example is the 'For the party in the interests of the people'? Is the 'For the people'. The equation is simple where, A=for the party = B for the people If A=B you have a perfect solution. Then selfishness can be counted as naught. It would be impossible for this to be the case always but we need to think about what is done for the sake of any political or other institution without being rushed to immediate solutions that don't work. It appears to me that we need to acknowledge which is being served and account for it. It is bringing the equation to mind that would make the difference. Political systems are difficult to control and the electorate can only ever glimpse at the amount of work that goes into running the country. It would make accountability easier. Sometimes policies don't work in the best interests of the public although they seem to answer variable needs. For example, in the NHS concentrating on getting waiting lists down does not necessarily guarantee the quality of the work! But it is a step in the right direction.

The electorate need to vote for their best policies and results and not for spinned personalities.

Unite the world.

The world is uniting in ways that have never been seen before. For the world to survive it own mistakes it needs to unite as a stable and united force. Thinking is changing in our age and as never before in the history of man, the world is beginning to take corporate responsibility for all its neighbours.

The recent LIVEAID8 revealed the current trend amongst the young people of today which is to provide justice and food for the poor. The Pop World has mobilized the forces of compassion in the world to produce a truly amazing message to those in power. That is that the world itself does not want millions of it's people living in poverty and worse.

There is often a lack of simple thought and imagination regarding the needs or regarding interpretation of rules and governance. There is too much to do and too much to think about to have the time to use imagination in a way that will free the resources that are wasted and send it to the parts of the world that need it. So, what tends to happen is that we ask the questions about resources before asking the questions about the need.

This is true in many institutions. Often the solution is within the system and easy to implement but it is the will to do so that is the problem. In my own area of work within the health service one sees it all the time. Energy and time are stretched so much that simple solutions that can make all the difference are not implemented. Sometimes there is no vision only the slavish meeting of demands. I think in the NHS we try and get it right and there are so many wonderful people but we need to think NEED MEET THE NEED. Not what do we have to do about it. Again the truth of the situation can lead to compassion and mercy and bring peace to many. I believe that the average man or woman in the street will help their neighbours. The world is generous. The problem is the lack of resources and lack of power to change things and the lack of belief that the average person in the street can change things.

I believe the main cause of disillusionment is the lack of involvement. The Electorate do not think their vote makes a difference or anything they say matters. I wish everyone could belong to a political party or something they believed in. Then the people would indeed be empowered. PeacePlease says find your values, live them and contribute to the world. Live TMLP.

8. PeacePlease and the International Scene

International co-operation has always been in place. After the First World War the United Nations was formed so that war would not be necessary. Undoubtedly the work of the UN has been and is vital for world security. This is the age of international cooperation and unity. The peace of the world depends on it and the ability of such organisations to accept and tolerate difference is of paramount importance.

There is something we can all do for peace. The UNA, a non-governmental organisation that supports the UN, coined the phrase the Culture of Peace. This is seen not just as something that politicians do but something that you and I and every single person does in their own lives in their own way. We need to see Society moving in the direction for support for the UN.

International Peace

Society begins for everyone in school, in the education system. It is in the classrooms that the beginning of a new consciousness has begun. One which says that aggression as a means of solving problems must change. However, we live in a world mind set that suggests that only war will work.

Solutions looked for are tainted by the need for quick concrete results. They include rapid reactions because of the demand for immediate solutions by a terrified public.

For the world to change we need a mind change that puts protects peaceful solutions. We have to create a mind set that says that what ever the problem the nation has needs and negotiation must work. This means that knee jerk reactions must go. The nail biting stuff from the Northern Ireland Peace Process showed what a painstaking labour intensive and difficult process it is. As intelligent human beings there has to be another way. We can solve the problems of the atoms of the universe we can solve the problems of war.

To those caught up in war all of this must seem pie in the sky. Once the first bullet has been fired and the first bomb dropped you set in motion a retaliation and a need for violence that is difficult draw back from. The battle is lost after the first shot or bomb. Certainly for the soldier the decision to be a soldier casts him or her into a role that trains him or her to respond and fight. I do not think the problem lies at that level, he or she can do no other than respond. I know from my meditation that the young men and women that serve in the forces of whatever nation are dear to God. The Great Universal Love extends to them and their sacrifice and I am sure God weeps for them. They deserve to live. So, how then can we have peace without warfare?

I believe it is possible but there needs to be a desire on both sides and a decision not to give an immediate military response. Having said that it seems unlikely that some religious and political groups will accept anything but an immediate response of power. By that I mean 'You do that to me and this is what I will do to you'. Patience and waiting is not normal for us in our society, where everything is done on a rapid basis. We have to be in a position to say that we can wait.

I find myself in a dilemma with my conviction that war does not work. Knowing the plight of those on the ground in war zones one cannot sometimes reconcile what one believes and the seemingly impossible quest of the armed forces in places like Afghanistan. I know if I were in danger there is no way I would not board a military Aircraft if was taking me to safety. However, I think we have to go on trying. The solution has to be through dialogue, somehow. It is also dangerous. I cannot imagine what it must be like to have been President Bush when he was informed that the two towers had fallen. Or what it must be like for to Tony Blair when faced with angry parents of dead soldiers. I cannot imagine either what it must really be like for the young soldiers faced with trying to bring peace to a region where the residents clearly don't want them and where death must seem an unfair price to pay for good will.

But to have a better way we must I believe try at the political level. My vision says stop the fighting. Is it possible faced with terrorism and insurgency by whatever side?

Psychological Preparation.

The amazing interactions of the NI peace process were about the preparation for meetings, the agendas and the maintenance of those meetings in the face of what appeared to be failure to reach a solution. That means meetings and cease fires for as long as it takes.

I believe that there is an unrecognized ingredient in war and that is that whole nations suffer from Post Traumatic Stress Disorder. That is, where the person re- lives the horror of life threatening situations.. When this happens the threat response grows and there is more likely to be a response of aggression. The feeling of threat is produced by the memory of the event

Sitting in a meeting for the Christians and Jews I heard the pain of those who had been involved or whose families had been involved in the holocaust. What I heard was, pain and trauma.

Nations need to help one another over the trauma. Cross border contact may help them to see that everyone is traumatised by war, even the enemy. We all need to be kind to each other. How can an Israeli look on an Arab with compassion when his memory is of family member being harmed by the Arab? How can an Arab look at a Jew and not feel anger when his family has been injured. Psychologically it is almost impossible not to feel aggression. This must be seen as a kind of national demise and crisis. Do the most traumatised run their countries. This must be recognised and taken into account. Enemies are people! Nations need healing and need to trust again. It may be that this can be taken into consideration some how and negotiations be geared to an understanding of what this does. Negotiators might be the few that are not traumatised. I don't believe that any group caught up in war cannot be so affected. We need therefore political solutions.

Weapons.

We need major changes in economic thought. The proliferation of weapons reinforces the need for the army. It reinforces the idea that in order to survive you have to have power in weapons and not negotiation. Then we have lost already the mind set to negotiate. As weapons bring in revenue they also herald war.

The idea of a nuclear deterrent is based on the idea that the only thing anyone responds to is the bigger threat. However we know that threat produces more threat and that it leads to aggression. The UN was founded on the basis that international co- operation which would lessen the likelihood of war. It's charter prevents nations going to war on a whim. With the proliferation of Nuclear Deterrents are we to assume the world a safer place?

This is based on the notion that threat works? The nation depends on war and remakes the need for it and what it gets are massive sales. Is our economy funded by war? This is not a stable situation. What is needed is a situation that reduces threat and the likelihood of war. The sad thing is we may get to into a situation where every country owns weapons of mass destruction whilst the poor die of hunger and the young lack opportunities to get out of poverty - this is then an uneasy peace. The security of the nation is hijacked and the need for threat gets bigger and bigger. Then there is more and more wasted wealth, instead of a stable system which takes positive action to decrease the reasons for war.

One understands instinctively that this is right but the reasoning appears as naive when war is seen as the only solution. It sounds ridiculous. It sounds and looks pathetic when contrasted with the scenes of rockets, armed vehicles and amazing looking jets that scream through the air almost seemingly saying 'I have the power'.

Whilst the development of wealth making with the poorer nations has begun and the development of new technology to increase production is beginning. We are beginning to see that it is not impossible to turn weapons into ploughs, energy into fuel, and land into food instead.

Our world is changing and there have been amazing steps forward by political negotiation and now thanks largely to the armed forces we do have 'talking' on the agenda. We need to recognize also that some countries have taken the bullets out of politics.

Ireland did it! Ireland won! We need them and we should celebrate them.

We also need the TMLP of the European Union, The Israeli Parliament, The Arab League, the African

Congress. We need the continenets of the world to say Yes to Peace and No to war.

One Bread and One Cup.

I know of a symbol of the world. There is a loaf of bread and a cup - one bread one world. A symbol of meal sharing the world over. We need to see our world as one family. Sharing what we know and leaving what we do not understand and can do without.

There is no one in this world who cannot contribute to world peace. Whether it be in a classroom or in a hospital or in a kitchen, on the street or in the corridors of power, everyone can live the Truth, the Mercy, The Love and the Peace. PeacePlease is for everyone. Let there be peace there is one world ln the beginning and the end. So, Please Let's stop the fighting.

Sue Sterling.

About the Author

I am Sue Sterling and I am Clinical Psychologist working in Devon with troubled people. I am also a member of United Nations Association. I believe world peace is possible If we prioritize enough – all of us on this planet.